HANDBOOK

COMBAT TERRORISM

FOREIGN AND DOMESTIC

STEPS AND PROCEDURES TO PROTECT YOURSELF

By Lenzy Kelley

Published By:
1stBooks
2511 West Third Street, Suit 1
Bloomington, IN 47404
http://www.1stbooks.com

ISBN: 1-58820-367-0

1stBooks - rev. 1/26/01

Table of Contents

PREFACE

This handbook is intended to provide information and suggestions to reduce the vulnerability to acts of terrorism.

In view of recent and continued high levels of terrorist activity, both foreign and domestic, it's become necessary to take appropriate measures to protect yourself from terroristic acts not only when traveling, but also on a day to day basis within your community and work environment. Recent terrorist acts (i.e., World Trade Center and Oklahoma Federal building) would suggest that terrorist acts are not confined to tourist centers. They can, will and have struck at the common work place. As such, no one is safe. With our everyday safety at peril, it is imperative that all of us become aware of our surroundings and take the necessary steps to be discussed in this handbook to protect ourselves against terrorist activities.

In Memory of Lenzy Kelley, Sr.

Chapter 1

Introduction

Every 17 days, terrorist strike against government officials and installations worldwide. During the past 15 years, terrorists have killed or maimed thousands of military personnel, public servants, businessmen, educators and clergy. Each year, the statistics get increasingly grim and the terrorist incidents become increasingly lethal.

In the past, the threat of terrorism came principally from two distinct ideologies, communism and Iranian Islamic fundamentalism. Both used terrorism as a form of warfare with knowledge that democracies, their main enemies, are especially vulnerable. However, with the collapse of the Soviet empire, terrorism from communist regimes has all but vanished, while terrorism from Islamic fundamentalist has increased dramatically.

The cost of terrorism goes far beyond the carnage and destruction caused by individual incidents. When the United States is the target of such actions, the cost of terrorism must be measured not only in loss of American life or damage to U.S. installations and property, but in less tangible though no less meaningful terms--loss of American credibility and a diminished capacity of the United States to influence international events.

Each terrorist attack--each bombing, each assassination, each incident that brings international humiliation to Free World institutions--undermines public confidence in the established government and erodes national resolve and faith in its leadership. The U. S. Defense Department responds to the terrorist threat and activities with two forms of positive actions:

- Counterterrorism
- Anti-terrorism

Both above cited actions will be discussed in a later chapter.

TERRORISM

Definition: Terrorism is the criminal use of violence or the threat of violence to attain goals, often political or ideological in nature, through fear, intimidation, or coercion. A terrorist act is usually dramatic and violent. It is often directed against a symbolic target and is intended to influence others, rather than the immediate victim. The serious effects of terrorism generated by local and international terrorist groups in many countries of the world and the demonstrated ability of some groups to operate across national boundaries have made terrorism an international problem.

CHARACTERISTICS:

1) Terrorist groups are not governed by time constraints. Preparation for conspiratorial terrorism can take months or even years, and most terrorist groups are psychologically prepared for protracted operations.

2) Terrorism is not limited by political borders. Many terrorist operate internationally.

3) Political terrorist groups are durable. Some organizations thought to have been destroyed or dispersed have revived in one form or another to pose renewed threats.

4) Most political terrorism is calculated and rational, not "mindless". Terrorists usually seek to create a

2

"credible threat" for political leverage. Their immediate objectives are mainly psychological: generation of fear among the populace, disruption within the government, and a general loss of confidence in the existing social order or government policies.

5) The more common types of violence committed by terrorist are bombings, hijacking, kidnapping and assassination; however, robbery of finance offices or weapons storage facilities play an important role in furthering terrorist objectives, and such acts are of particular concern to government agencies and personnel.

6) Terrorists conceal their explosive/incendiary devices in vehicles and containers such as travel bags, suitcases, backpacks etc.

7) Terrorists carefully reconnoiter any target they intend to attack.

8) Terrorists seek to adapt their appearance to the given surroundings. They could try for instance to gain access in uniforms of police or in ambulances using appropriate vehicles. Many terrorists are females!

9) Terrorists always carry arms and once in a critical situation use them recklessly!

CHAPTER 2

Legacy of Terror

TERRORIST ACTS:

The following is not all conclusive of terrorist acts committed worldwide:

Jan. 24, 1975: New York's Fraunces Tavern was bombed by a terrorist group seeking Puerto Rican independence, killing four people and injuring 53.

Dec. 29, 1975: A bomb in the main passenger terminal of LaGuardia Airport kills 11 people and injures 70.

Sept. 11, 1976: A bomb left by Croatian terrorist in the Grand Central IRT station kills a police bomb expert and wounds three others.

1981: Anwar Sadat, president of Egypt, assassinated at military parade by group of Islamic fundamentalist who are violently opposed to the peace process with Israel.

April 18, 1983: The U.S. Embassy in Beirut, Lebanon, is almost totally destroyed by a car-bomb explosion that kills 63 people, including 17 Americans, Pro-Iranian terrorists are blamed.

Oct. 23, 1983: The U.S. Marine headquarters in Beirut, Lebanon, is destroyed when a truck loaded with explosives blows up outside building, killing 241 Marine and Navy personnel.

April 2, 1986: An Arab terrorist group bombs a TWA jet flying from Rome to Athens, killing four American passengers, including a baby. Nine others are injured.

April 5, 1986: A Libyan terrorist bombing at a West Berlin Disco kills a U.S. soldier, a Turkish woman and wounds 155 others, including 60 Americans.

Sept. 25, 1986: The South African Consulate on Park Avenue is bombed. There are no fatalities.

Sept. 26, 1986: A shadowy terrorist group calling itself the United Freedom Front bombs a Union Carbide plant in Westchester county. There were no injuries. Police say the group is responsible for at least 14 other similar bombings from 1984 to 1986.

1987: Palestinian uprising, known as the Intifadeh, erupts in Gaza refugee camp and spreads to West Bank. Over the next several years some 2,000 Palestinians, including collaborators with Israel, and hundreds of Israelis are killed.

Dec. 21, 1988: Pan Am Flight 103 is blown out of the sky over Lockerbie, Scotland. Libyan terrorists have been blamed for the bombing, which killed all 270 passengers aboard the New York-bound airliner.

March 1988: Three Palestinian terrorists seize a bus taking workers to a nuclear plant and shoot three

Israelis dead before troops storm the bus and kill the gunmen.

July 1989: A Palestinian terrorist grabs the wheel of a bus and sends it plunging into a ravine, killing at least 14 and injuring 27.

February 1990: Arab terrorists attack a bus packed with Israeli tourists in Egypt and kill at least 12 and wound 21.

March 1992: A knife wielding Muslim man goes on a rampage in Jaffa during the holy day of Purim, killing one Israeli and one Palestinian and wounding 20.

Feb. 26, 1993: Muslim fundamentalists bomb the World Trade Center, killing six people, injuring more than 1,000 and causing $550 million in damages.

Feb. 25, 1994: Jewish settler Baruch Goldstein shoots dead kneeling Arab worshippers in a mosque in Hebron in the West Bank, killing at least 29 before survivors beat him to death.

April 1994: Arab car-bomber kills eight people and injures 44 in attack in Israel

April 13, 1994: Palestinian blows himself up on bus in Hadera in central Israel. Six Israelis killed, 25 wounded. Hamas claims responsibility.

October 1994: Hamas Islamic Resistance Movement bomber Saleh Abdel-Rahim al-Souwi kills himself and 22 other people in suicide bomb attack on Israeli bus in Tel Aviv.

Nov. 12, 1994: Palestinian suicide bomber in the Gaza Strip kills three Israeli soldiers. Hamas-related group, Islamic Jihad, claims responsibility.

Dec. 25, 1994: Palestinian blows up bus in Jerusalem, wounding 12 Israelis. Hamas claims responsibility.

Jan 22, 1995: Two Islamic Jihad suicide bombers kill 21 Israelis, all but one of them soldiers, in explosions that rip through a bus stop at Beit Lid near Netanya in central Israel.

April, 1995: Alisa Flatow, a 20 year-old college student from West Orange, N.J., and seven Israeli soldiers were killed in a suicide-bombing attack on a bus traveling through the Gaza Strip.

July, 1995: Six people are killed when a massive bomb is detonated by a suicide bomber outside Tel Aviv.

August, 1995: Joan Davenny, a teacher from Woodbridge, Conn., is one of five people killed in the bombing of a bus in Jerusalem.

October 1995: Fathi Shiqaqi, leader of the Islamic Holy War movement, gunned down at a seaside resort in Malta by two men believed to be connected to the Israeli intelligence service.

Feb. 25, 1996: Palestinian suicide bombers strike in Jerusalem and Ashkelon, killing 25 people, including two Americans, and wounding more than 80. Hamas claims responsibility.

Feb. 26,1996: Arab-American drives rental car into Jerusalem bus stop, killing one Israeli, wounding 23. The driver, who is shot and killed, appears to be acting on his own, but Hamas claims responsibility.

Mar. 3, 1996: Bus bomb in Jerusalem kills at least 19 people, including six Romanians, two Palestinians and the suicide bomber. At least 10 people were wounded.

Mar. 1997: Suicide bomber kills himself and two other people at a Tel Aviv café.

Apr. 18, 1996: Gunmen open fire with automatic rifles at Europa Hotel near the Pyramids in Cairo, killing 18 Green tourist and wounding 16 others. An Egyptian also is wounded.

Sept. 18, 1997: Attackers throw firebombs and open fire on tourist bus outside the Egyptian Museum in downtown Cairo; killing 10 people many of them German tourist. Police say three foreigners and 15 Egyptians are wounded. El-Ulla, who days earlier walked out of the mental asylum where he had been committed for the 1993 killings and his brother, Mahmound, are sentenced to death for the attack.

Mar. 22, 1997: Three Israelis die 60 hurt by Tel Aviv bomb.

Nov. 1997: Two Americans shot to death in Karachi Pakistan.

Nov. 18, 1997: Islam radicals opened fire on tourists in Egypt, killing 61 people.

Feb. 14, 1998: China: bus Bombed in Wuhan.

Feb. 20, 1998: Toxic Terrorist plot attack.

Mar. 26, 1998: Four American and an Italian Citizen Kidnapped by Guerrillas in Columbia.

Apr. 1, 1998: Hamas Explosives Expert Dies in Blast.

Apr. 25, 1998: Shining Path Leaders Captured.

Apr. 28, 1998: 40 People Dead in Latest Algerian Massacre.

May 3, 1998: Firebomb Attacks in Amman.

May 25, 1998: Dissident Students Hijack Airline in Pakistan.

June 27, 1998: Suspects in World Trade Center Bombing Arrested in Thailand.

June 28, 1998: Islamic Militants Planned to Kidnap Americans in Egypt.

July 12, 1998: Rush-hour Bombing Foiled in London.

Aug.1, 1998: Car Bomb Detonated in Northern Ireland Shopping District.

Aug. 7, 1998: U.S. Embassies in East Africa Hit by Bomb Blasts.

Sept. 12, 1998: Sri Lanka Bomb Kills Mayor, Top Military Officers.

Oct. 3, 1998: Tamil Rebels Blamed for Sri Lankan Plane Crash.

Oct 30, 1998: Turkish Hijacking ends with Death of Hijacker.

Nov. 27, 1998: Bomb Explodes on Turkish Bus.

Dec. 1, 1998: Kurdish Suicide Bomber Injures 14 in Southeast Turkey.

Dec 29, 1998: Four Western Hostages Killed in Yemeni Rescue.

Jan. 2, 1999: Car Bomb in South Africa Injures Two.

Jan. 3. 1999: Ten Die in Grenade Attack in Philippines.

Jan. 28, 1999: Eleven Injured in Cape Town Bombing.

Feb. 24, 1999: First Real IRA Suspect Charged in Omagh Bombing.

Mar. 1, 1999: Three Americans Kidnapped in Colombia.

Mar. 2, 1999: Eight Tourists Killed in Uganda.

Mar. 5, 1999: Three Killed in Car Bomb in Turkey.

Mar. 14, 1999: Arson Attack Kills 13 in Istanbul Department Store.

Mar. 18, 1999: Four Killed in Suicide Bombing in Sri Lanka.

Mar. 19, 1999: Over 60 Dead in Bomb Blast at Russian Market.

Mar. 22, 1999: American Banks in Athens Hit By Blasts.

Apr. 11, 1999: Senior Iranian Commander Assassinated, Mujahedeen e-Khalq Claims Responsibility.

Apr. 13, 1999: Colombian Rebels Hijack Domestic Airliner.

Apr. 20, 1999: Neo-Nazi Group Claims London Blast.

May 31, 1999: Colombian Rebels Kidnap Entire Congregation.

June 22, 1999: At Least Ten Killed in blast at Indian Railway Station.

July 5, 1999: One Dead and More than Twenty Injured in Istanbul Bombing.

July 28, 1999: Bus Bombing in Kashmir Kills 11.

Aug. 1, 1999: FARC Car Bomb Kills Ten in Colombia.

Aug. 2, 1999: FARC Attack on Police Station Kills 17.

Aug. 4, 1999: Sri Lanka Convoy Attacked by LTTE Suicide Bomber.

Aug. 5, 1999: Terrorist Attack in Yemeni Market Kills Five.

Aug. 15, 1999: Western Tourists Kidnapped in Iran.

Sept. 16, 1999: Car Bomb Hits Apartment Block in Southern Russia.

Oct. 25, 1999: Japanese Hostages Released in Tajikistan.

Nov. 12, 1999: Rockets Fired at U.S. and U.N. Offices in Islamabad.

Nov. 29, 1999: Scores Injured in Cape Town Restaurant Bombing.

Dec. 18, 1999: Sri Lankan President Injured in Blast.

Jan. 3, 2000: Russian Embassy in Beirut Attacked.

Jan 5, 2000: LTTE Suicide Bomber Kills 13 in Sri Lanka.

Jan 21, 2000: ETA Car Bombing Kills Spanish Army Officer.

Feb. 23, 2000: Two Killed in ETA Car Bombing.

Mar. 5, 2000: Kidnappings of Cyclist, Electricity Workers in Colombia.

Apr. 27, 2000: Resort Hostages Held on Jolo Island.

May 7, 2000: Killing of Spanish Journalist Blamed on ETA.

Terrorists Act's continued:

MAIL BOMB BLITZ AT U.N.

TERROR IN ISRAEL
BOMBS KILL 13 AT MARKET
HAMAS: Release prisoners or more will die

Nail-packed bombs
Spill river of blood

14 hurt as pipe bombs explode in busy Tel Aviv

6 injured in abortion clinic bomb blasts

52 survive ditching of hijacked plane

Egyptian Embassy bombed in Pakistan

U.S. TARGETED FOR TERROR

JFK plot part of Hamas campaign

CIA chief sees surge in terror

2 suicide bombers kill 25 in Israel

Truck bomb kills 53

1,000 hurt in blast, Sri Lanka rebels blamed

Israel Blast kills 6

Bomb leaves rage, horror

Notorious terrorist is sought

Paris subway blast kills 4

Algerian terrorists linked to train bomb

Saudis make sketch of bombing suspect

FBI: 'FOREIGN COUNTRY' BEHIND SAUDI BOMB

9 ISRAELIS INJURED IN LEBANON SUICIDE BLAST

17

Terrorist car bomb kills 4 at Peru hotel

Explosion on Philippine plane kills one

Muslim group claims responsibility and warns other planes will be hit

MAN SEIZES 27 KOREANS IN MOSCOW

COMMANDOS ATTACK; ALL ON BUS ARE FREED

TERROR IN OKLAHOMA CITY
DEATH AND DESTRUCTION AS BOMB ROCKS OKLA.
MAYOR PUTS APPLE ON RED ALERT

TERRORISTS TAMPER WITH TRACK
ARIZONA TRAIN PLUNGES INTO GORGE - 1 DEAD, SCORES HURT

5 YANKS KILLED, 34 HURT IN SAUDI TERROR BLAST

MFO Director Killed by Terrorists
SECURITY FORCES are searching for the killers of the director general of the Multinational Force and Observers in the Sinai, who was shot and killed in Rome February 15 by a suspected terrorist.

'War' declared after latest bomb kills 19

TERRORIST ORGANIZATIONS

Muslim Brotherhood - Egypt

Islamic Salvation Front - Algeria

Islamic Armed Group - Algeria

Hamas - PLO/Iranian

Izz el-Deenal-Qassam Brigades - Military Arm of Hamas

Islamic Jihad - PLO/Iranian

Shining Path - Puru (Pro Myoist)

Tupac Amaros - Puru (Pro Cuban)

Harkat-Ul-Ansar - India

Gestoppo Bros - USA

Huzbulla - PLO/Iranian

Al-Faran - Kashmiri separatists - India

Tamil Separatists - Sri Lanka

Basque Separatists, Herri Batasuna – Spain

We Who Built Sweden – Sweden

Animal Secret Committee - Pakistan

Abu Sayyaf Group (ASG) – Philippines

Al-Gama'a al-Islamiya (The Islamic Group, IG)- Egypt

Al-Qa'ida (the Base) – Afghanistan

Aum Shinrikyo – Japan

Chukaku-Ha (Nucleus or Middle Core Faction – Japan

Democratic Front for the Liberation of Palestine (DFLP) – Palestinian

Fatah – Revolutionary Council (Abu Nidal Organization) – Lebanon

Hamas (Islamic Resistance Movement)- Palestinian

Harakat ul-Mujahedin (HUM) – Pakistan

Hizballah (Party of God) – Lebanon

Irish Republican Army (IRA) – Northern Ireland

Jamaat ul-Fuqra – Pakistan

Japanese Red Army (JRA) – Japan

Jihad Group – Egypt

Kach and Kahane Chai – Isreal

Kurdistan Worker's Party (PKK) – Turkey

Lautaro Youth Movement (MJL) – Chile

Loyalist Volunteer Force (LVF) – Northern Ireland

Manuel Rodriquez Patriotic Front (FPMR)- Chile

Moranzanist Patriotic Front (FPM) – Honduras

Mujahedin-e Khalq Organization (MEK or MKO) – Iran

National Liberation Army (ELN) Columbia – Columbia

Nestor Paz Zamora Commission (CNPZ) – Bolivia

New People's Army (NPA) – Philippines

Palestine Liberation Front (PLF) – Iraq

Palestine Islamic Jihad (PIJ) – Palestinian

Party of Democratic Kampuchea (Khmer Rouge) – Cambodia

Popular Front for the Liberation of Palestine (PFLP) – Palestinian

Popular Front for the Liberation of Palestine – General – Palestinian

Popular Struggle Front (PSF) – Syria

Qibla and People Against Gangsterism and Drugs (PAGAD) – South Africa

Real IRA – Northern Ireland

Red Army Faction (RAF) – Germany

Red Brigades (BR) – Italy

Revolutionary Armed Forces of Colombia (FARC) – Colombia

Revolutionary Organization 17 November – Greece

Revolutionary People's Liberation Party/Front (DHCP/F) – Turkey

Revolutionary People's Struggle (ELA) – Greece

The above listing does not cite all terrorist organizations. However, if you travel to any of the countries listed, you need to be aware that these organizations exist and act accordingly.

The preceding articles and headlines denoting terrorists actions and organizations have unfortunately became extremely familiar. To combat terrorist acts and organizations, governments world-wide have implemented anti-terrorism and counter-terrorism actions. Those actions are defined as follows:

"Anti-terrorism--actions that reduce the vulnerability of people and facilities, such as barriers, gates, armed guards travel, visa controls, and personal habits. Recent terrorists acts directed at US personnel and resources at home and overseas reinforce the need for adequate anti-terrorism planning. The term "anti-terrorism" is used to denote those defensive measures personnel can take to reduce their vulnerability.

"Counter-terrorism - actions initiated by Governments to combat terrorism. Those actions include intelligence gathering, sharing intelligence with other countries, enhanced personnel training apprehension of terrorists, and infiltration of terrorists organizations.

Specific anti-terrorist and counter terrorists precautions will be addressed in Chapter 3.

BOMB THREAT PROCEDURES

A. MAIL BOMBS

1. Unfortunately, the deadly ingredients required for mail bombs are easy to acquire. It took an investigative news team less than a half-hour to purchase the items required for a simple but deadly detonating device--with guidance from the Anarchists Cook-book". Total cost, $11.00.
2. Experts state that in most cases you don't have to look past your supermarket, kitchen sink or tool box

to find items such as pipe, cigar boxes, electrical cord, small screws and nine-volt batteries.

3. Gunpowder would be the most expensive ingredient to buy and also the most difficult to acquire. In most states, it's against the law t sell gunpowder, However, it can be found in the form of 10 powerful M-180 firecrackers -- roughly the equivalent of 2 and 1/2 sticks of dynamite.

4. Smokeless gunpowder, the type used by the Unabomber, can be legally purchased for about $15 a pound. It is considered a low explosive and doesn't require a basting cap, which is a tightly regulated item

5. If all of the ingredients purchased by the news team had been assembled, all it would have take to set the device off would have been an electrical charge or flame. This author does not advise anyone to try it -- it is both extremely dangerous and illegal. Anyone caught with such a device would face a felony weapons possession charge -- which carries maximum penalty of 8 and 1/3 to 25 years in jail in most states.

   a. *Identification Features.* Deadly bombs come in all shapes, colors, methods of delivery, big and small packages. Investigators say there's no way to guard against becoming the target of a mail bomber -- but there are ways to avoid turning victim. Postal authorities say bomb-laden letters and packages often bear tell-tale signs that should alert recipients to trouble. (See figures 1 & 2)

      • Mail bombs may be marked "personal" or private -- something to pay attention to when the addressee usually doesn't get

personal mail at the office (unusual restricted endorsement).
- The person's name or title may be inaccurate.
- There may be no return address or it may be fictitious (sender is unknown).

You can always call the post office and see if the address exists before you open it. I it doesn't exist, you know you've got a major problem on your hands.

- Watch out for protruding wires, aluminum foil or string. Foil prevents the electrical circuit from being completed. Once it is removed the circuit is completed and the bomb can be detonated.
- Peculiar odors and buzzing, ticking or sloshing sounds should set off some alarms.
- Take note of any postmark that differs from the return address.
- Be leery if there's more postage than the package warrants.
- Mail bombers add extra postage in order to avoid dealing with window clerks.

Anyone suspicious about a letter or package should leave it unopened, evacuate the area and open windows in order to speed ventilation.

- Letters feel rigid, appear uneven or lopsided, or are bulkier than normal.
- May have oil stains on the wrapper.

- Address is prepared to insure anonymity of sender homemade labels, cut and past lettering).
- Handwriting appears distorted, with mis-spelling.
- Pressure or resistance is noted when removing contents.
- Several combinations of tape are used to sure the bundle.

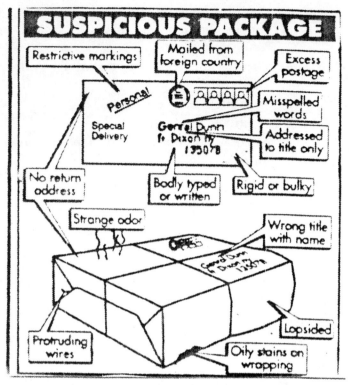

Telltale signs of lethal mailings

Signs that could raise suspicions about a letter or package, according to the FBI:

- Excessive postage.
- Incorrect titles of the addressees.
- No names of addressees.
- Misspellings of common words.
- Oily stains or discolorations.
- No return address.
- Excessive weight.
- Rigid envelope.
- Lopsided or uneven envelope.
- Protruding wires or tin foil.
- Visual distractions.
- Foreign mail, air mail and special delivery.
- Restrictive markings such as "confidential" and "personal."
- Handwritten or poorly typed addresses.
- Excessive securing material such as masking tape, string, etc.

Figure 1

ANATOMY OF A CARD BOMB

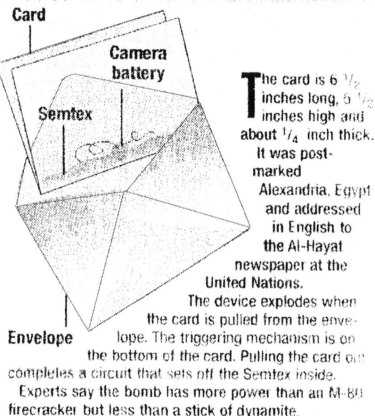

Card

Camera battery

Semtex

Envelope

The card is 6 ½ inches long, 5 ½ inches high and about ¼ inch thick. It was post-marked Alexandria, Egypt and addressed in English to the Al-Hayat newspaper at the United Nations.

The device explodes when the card is pulled from the envelope. The triggering mechanism is on the bottom of the card. Pulling the card out completes a circuit that sets off the Semtex inside.

Experts say the bomb has more power than an M-80 firecracker but less than a stick of dynamite.

It can maim or even kill the person who opens it.

Figure 2

- Unprofessionally wrapped parcel is endorsed "Fragile-Handle with Care" or "Rush-Do not Delay"
- Package makes a buzzing or ticking noise.
- Use of excessive amounts of securing material (i.e., tape, string, glue, etc.).
- Package is designed to be or indicates only one method of opening.
- Letter/package addressed to CEO, President or Head of Corporation.
- Letter/Package addressed to 1st Floor addressee.

B. NEW RULES FOR MAILING PACKAGES

The Postal Service has announced restrictions designed to keep mail bombs form making their way aboard commercial airliners.

Customers will have to take packages weighing more than one pound to a post office or hand them directly to a carrier.

Non-local parcels that are dropped in collection boxes may be returned to sender.

The new restrictions are currently in effect. "The U.S. mail flies on commercial airlines everyday."

The new rules do not apply to Express Mail or private carriers, which do not use commercial airlines.

Metered mail, which has an identification number coded in the stamp, is not included in the restriction.

C. TELEPHONIC BOMB THREATS

In the event of a telephonic warning call that a bomb or other incendiary device has been placed, the person making the call may reveal information that could help identify him or her and also locate the incendiary device. As such, the person receiving the call should take the following actions:

1. Remain calm, gather as much information as possible.
2. Alert a co-worker while the caller is still on the line.
3. The co-worker using another phone should notify the police.
4. After notifying the police, the co-worker should then notify a supervisor and other workers. The supervisor will make the decision to begin evacuating the building.
5. During the evacuation, employees should take all personal belongings i.e., bags, purses).
6. Stay off the phone.
7. During evacuation do not touch any suspicious objects.
8. Make note of any strange objects, deserted packages or out of place materials.
9. If a suspected bomb is found, do not pick up or touch. Note the location and provide information to police.
10. During evacuation, do not congregate in a large group in one area (i.e. parking lot). Move away from the building (300 meters) in small groups at different locations.
11. While the co-worker is busy contacting the police and notifying other employees to evacuate the building, the called party should make note of the following:

Caller's Voice:

Calm	Distinct	Cracking voice
Angry	Slurred	Disguise
Excited	Nasal	Accent
Slow	Stutter	Familiar
Rapid/Fast	Lisp	Whispered
Soft	Raspy	High Pitched
Loud	Deep	Intoxicated
Laughter	Ragged	Pleasant
Crying	Clearing throat	Distorted
Normal	Deep breathing	

12. If voice is familiar, who did it sound like?

Background Sounds:

Street noises	Office Machinery
Internal from within	Crockery
Factory Machinery	Booth
Voices	Animal noises Trains
PA System	Clear/Quiet Airplanes
Music	Static Party atmosphere
House noises	Local Mixed
Motor	Long distance Bedlam
Other	

Threat Language:

Well spoken (educated)	Poor
Foul	Incoherent
Irrational	Taped
Fair	Message read by threat maker
Good	

34

Accent:

Local   Not Local
Regional   Foreign
Race

Caller's Manner:

Calm   Angry
Rational   Irrational
Coherent   Incoherent
Deliberate   Emotional
Righteous   Laughing
Crying

Caller's Identity:

Sex:
     Male or Female
Adult   Juvenile
Approximate Age   Exact wording of threat.

13. Keep caller talking. Pretend difficulty with your hearing, If caller seems agreeable to further conversation, ask questions like:

- *When will it go off? Certain Hour--Time Remaining--What kind of bomb? Where are you now? How do you know so much about the bomb?--What is your name and address? Where is it right now? What does it look like?--What will cause it to explode?--Did you place the bomb?--(If yes) Why did you do it?--Who or what do you represent?*

14. If building is occupied, inform caller that detonation could cause injury or death. Note, if caller appears familiar with plant or building by his description of the bomb location?

35

15. Building should be completely evacuated 30 minutes prior to the time in which the bomb is scheduled to detonate, if information is provided by caller (30 minute rule).
16. As a finale note to telephonic bomb threats, with today's technology, an activity agency can have the local phone company install "caller ID" as a feature to your phone system. The caller ID feature will replace the archaic method of soliciting the phone company in an attempt to trace the call, before the caller hangs up.

Evacuation

A. EVACUATION

1. Several important aspects of evacuation were previously discussed in Chapter 3. For re-enforcement, they will be repeated. During a bomb threat, supervisors or activity directors (who ever is in charge) should immediately evaluate the seriousness before making the decision to evacuate the entire building or specific areas.
2. During building evacuation, the fire alarm should be sounded and fire evacuation procedures implemented. If you don't have fire evacuation procedures for your building, get in touch with the local fire department, they will be glad to assist you in preparing building specific evacuation procedures. To assist the bomb disposal unit, the building diagram or lay-out should be made available.

3. Moving a large number of people under emergency conditions is a hazardous undertaking unless ABSOLUTE control is maintained. Thus, particular attention should be given to planning evacuation procedures. At first though, immediate and total evacuation would seem to be the most appropriate response to any bomb threat; however, there are significant economic and safety factors that may weigh against the evacuation. Even where evacuation is possible and desirable, the process itself may not be as simple as it might appear.

4. In evacuating any building, people must be routed through the most public areas of the building-- corridors and stairwells--and these are the areas that are most likely to contain an explosive or incendiary device.

1. As such, considerations must be given to routes of evacuation and priorities for removing people from a building when a bomb threat is received. Routes and priorities established will be based on the type of building and the location of people within the building. Persons to act as guides to lead the evacuation and to control the people during exit must be predesignated and trained. Routes and priorities established will also depend on the type of building and the location of people in relation to the area in which the bomb is located. In multi-story buildings, rooms or floors above the danger point and immediately blow should be evacuated first. Also, on the same floor, evacuate 3 rooms away on all sides.

6. Before giving the order to evacuate, the person(s) in charge should consider the following:

The caller - What did he say?
Did the caller sound serious in his threats?

Has this been a recurring thing?
Are employees excused from work when such threats are experienced?
Is it possible that this call was precipitated by new reports or other calls?
Will immediate evacuation of the premises expose personnel to greater danger?
What is the size of the building; how many people are involved?

7. A bomb threat plan should be in place prior to a bomb threat. The bomb threat plan should outline the following:

    Key Personnel --
    Building Bomb Marshall
    Building Coordinators
    Evacuation Guides

    Evacuation Plan
    Phone Numbers for Key Personnel
    Phone Numbers for Police and Bomb Disposal Unit
    Phone Numbers for Fire Department and Local Hospital

8. When preparing the bomb threat plan, other areas and questions to consider are as follows:

    a. *Who has the authority to order evacuation?* The supervisor of the building concerned.
    b. *Who makes the decision to permit reentry into the building following a search in which no bomb is found?*

c. *How will evacuation be signaled?* Establish a signal for evacuation and proceed according to pre-established evacuation plan.

d. *If evacuation is ordered, what procedures will be followed?* Evacuation teams should be designated to guide the occupants out of the area. Alternative evacuation routes must be provided, preferably the same routes used in case of fire.

e. *Who will be part of the evacuation team?* These people should be designated before the incident and thoroughly trained. Areas through which evacuation will proceed should be searched and cleared before evacuation. These include areas inside and outside the threatened building. Public areas are the most likely places for a bomb to be located and are the usual avenues of exit. The evacuation team should be able to control the evacuation and eliminate panic that could lead to injuries.

f. *To what areas do you evacuate the occupants?* Occupants should be evacuated to an area at least 300 feet away from the threatened area. It must be emphasized that the 300 foot figure is a minimum. Greater distances are encouraged, if at all possible. In any case, evacuees should be instructed to take cover and shelter from possible fragmentation.

g. *What are the responsibilities of the occupants during evacuation?* The occupants should open all doors and windows. This will reduce the shock effect of the bomb. Electrical units should be unplugged to reduce the chance of detonation and to reduce noise from an audio check. Then they should proceed calmly, following the orders if the evacuation team. Take personal belongings. Don't touch suspicious objects.

Note: Managers should appoint someone as the facility Bomb Threat Coordinator. Get that person trained and have that person train the remainder of the workforce as to how to re-act to a Bomb threat.

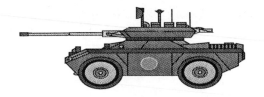

CHAPTER 3

Steps to Take to Avoid Becoming a Victim of Terrorism

Broadly defined, steps taken to combat terrorism and to avoid becoming a victim of terrorism can be called counter-terrorism and anti-terrorist measures. The following represents recommended anti-terrorist precautions that individuals can personally implement in an effort to reduce their vulnerability:

- Encourage security awareness in your family and discuss what to do if your security is threatened.
- Be alert for surveillance attempts and suspicious persons or activities; report them to the proper authorities. Remember, most terrorist attacks occur near the victim's home or office.
- Vary your personal routine; be as unpredictable as possible in your comings and goings.
- Check in with friends and family; let them know where you are or when to expect you.
- Always carry change for the telephone. Know the emergency numbers for police, fire ambulance and hospital.

- Know where to find civilian police, military police, government agencies and other safe locations.
- Avoid public disputes or confrontations. Report any trouble to the proper authorities.
- Set up simple signals to alert family members or associates to danger.
- Carry identification showing your blood type and any special medical conditions. Keep one week's supply of essential medication on hand.
- Keep a low profile. Shun publicity. Don't flash your cash.
- Avoid revealing your home address, phone number or any information about family -- unless you have good reason.
- Keep your personal affairs in order. Keep wills current, have power of attorney drawn up and ensure family financial security.
- When going our for any reason, avoid going along. Try to travel with at lease one other person - there is safety in numbers. However, individuals should avoid forming groups of more than 3 or 4 persons when in public and when possible, should not use automobiles which identify them as Americans, or official representatives of the US Government. If possible, locally-produced cars or a commonly used color and model should be used
- Travel only on busy, well-traveled thoroughfares, staying away from isolated back-country roads. Avoid known dangerous areas.
- Shun publicity-especially the local news media. It is important that the home address and telephone numbers be safeguarded, along with other personal and background information on family members.

- Do not get involved with local politics (as did Lori Berenson, currently serving a prison term in Peru for helping the TUPAC communist terrorist group plan an attack on the Peruvian Congress).

- Never leave your wallet or purse unattended. When asked for identification give only the information requested. Never surrender your entire wallet or card case. Check credit cards periodically. And, if you make a large local purchase, notice to see if you are being following.

- Walk on well-lit, heavily-traveled streets. Avoid shortcuts through alleys. Stay in the middle of the sidewalk. If you are threatened from a car, run in the opposite direction to seek help. If you are approached by a suspicious person, cross the street or change directions.

- Use well-lighted bus stops and observe fellow passengers. If you think you are being followed, walk into a store or police department and report the incident. Attempt to identify the individual.

- In buildings-use elevators. Do not risk attack in a poorly-lit stairwell. Stand near the elevator control panel and, if threatened, push the alarm button.

- Never leave keys or valuables in coat pockets. Use discretion in revealing personal plans during conversations.

- Never pick up hitchhikers.

- Lock your car no matter how shot a time it might be left unattended. If it necessary to leave car keys with a parking attendant, leave only the ignition key.

- Gas tanks should be maintained at least half-full with a locked gas cap.

- When parking your vehicle, try to arrange to part in a locked garage or protected area. If this is not possible, at least try to park the vehicle off the street.
- On multiple-lane highways, drive toward the center of the road to make it more difficult for your car to be forced to the curb.
- While in your car, keep all doors locked, windows closed or slightly opened.
- If the car breaks down in an unfamiliar area, raise the hood and trunk and remain inside with the doors locked and windows up. Do not trust offered assistance; ask anyone who offers assistance to call the police.
- Never leave for work at the same time.
- Give no clues that you are about to leave.
- Do not leave by the same door
- Do not follow a pattern in your use of alternate doors.
- Have your car kept in a secure place overnight to prevent the attachment of a bomb.
- Know who cleans your house or office and has access to your phones.
- Watchout for unexplained or unfamiliar containers in your work area.
- Learn what a bomb looks like and what packaging it may come in.
- Learn your company's procedures for reporting a bomb threat.
- Knowledge of the host country can be a valuable aid in avoiding a terrorist incident. Anyone not familiar with the language of the host country should learn certain key phrases that include phrases that may mean something derogatory in the

host country language. One should also learn how to use both public and private telephones in case of emergencies. Finally, stay abreast of foreign advisories to enhance your awareness of the political climate of the host country.

For US military personnel and government officials:

- Avoid travel to areas of high treat unless it's mission essential.
- Before traveling through high-threat areas and high-risk, airports review the Department of Defense code of conduct guidance for personnel subject to terrorist activity.
- At your nearest US Embassy or Consulate, ask the regional security officer about current security concerns where you intend to travel; get briefed on precautionary measures.
- Use military aircraft or Air Mobility Command Charter when you travel in high-threat areas.
- Avoid wearing military uniforms or identification on commercial aircraft in high-threat areas or high-risk airports.
- Look and act like a civilian.
- Avoid clothing that is distinctively American or Western.
- Wear nondescript civilian clothing on commercial flights. Avoid wearing clothes that are clearly of US origin, such as cowboy hats. Blend with other passengers; don't stand out.
- Wear civilian clothing, even on military aircraft, if you're making connections with a commercial flight that will go through a high-risk area.

- Send classified material through approved channels. Carry it only if your mission requires you to.
- Avoid writing your military rank on travel documents.
- Avoid marking baggage with your military rank, insignia or duty station.
- Avoid public areas of the airport; proceed quickly through security checkpoints to await your next flight in a secure area.
- Avoid discussing your military affiliation with anyone.
- Remember that all hijackers may not reveal themselves at the same time; a lone hijacker may draw out security personnel to be neutralized by other hijackers.
- Show your tourist passport for identification, but remember that a tourist passport is only a shallow cover for your DOD affiliation.
- Make a habit of checking any vehicle you are about to enter. Though the threat of car bombs in the United States is relatively low, the discipline of taking precautions will serve you well if you should ever be stationed in a high threat area.
- Lock your vehicle when you leave it. Use a locking gas cap for security against foreign objects being placed in your fuel tank.
- Check around and under your vehicle before you enter for suspicious objects, wires or stains on the pavement. Look for signs of forced entry around the doors, windows, trunk, and hood.
- If your check reveals anything amiss, do not enter the vehicle.
- At work safeguard all travel itineraries.
- Do not display travel dates on desk calendars.

- Do not display daily calendars of senior officials and deny access of such information with a need-to-know.
- Conference and meeting agendas should not contain movement information.

When checking visitors at your office or facility check persons and vehicles carefully! CAUTION!! TERRORISTS ALSO HAVE SERVICE PASSES, ID CARDS, ETC.

- Have the document handed to you and ask for details which the true holder must know!
- Ask visitors for their destination and check if they are being expected there!
- Keep people and vehicles moving
- If any suspicion arises also check additional documents (registration certificate for POV). Match person to vehicle.

Look out for persons moving about conspicuously, taking notes or pictures, or using binoculars, in the vicinity of your office or facility.

- Take note of the description of any such suspicious persons and their vehicles!
- Note down the license number of any vehicle used!
- Report your observations at once!

Look out for parked vehicles and abandoned objects in the immediate vicinity and at some distance!

- Do not touch!
- Report at once!

- Fixed buildings and facilities should have layered defenses that push the defensive perimeter away from the hub of a facility.
- The first security obstacle a terrorist encounters should be at a sufficient distance from the target to allow immediate layers to close up and render the threat harmless.
- Employ reinforced concrete barriers and/or movable gates.
- Guards/Security forces can no longer afford to be ceremonial. They must be able to shoot to kill a selected oncoming target approaching at high speed through a crowd of innocent by-standers.
- They must remain disciplined and alert, regardless of the tedium associated with security.
- If any facility allows for an extended approach by vehicles, disguised reinforced obstacles should be installed to defeat the possibility of a vehicle accelerating with the intent of mounting steps to force an entry.

In your home, restrict the number of keys to your house, and change the locks if a key is lost. Lock all entrances, including the garage, even when you are home. Know your neighbors and keep a watch on each other's homes. Don't attract undue attention through loud parties and music. Check the identification of all public utility persons before allowing them inside. Do not allow uninvited strangers into your home.

Remain alert to strangers in your neighborhood, and write the license number and description of unknown vehicles in the area. Treat with suspicion any inquiries as to the whereabouts of other family members. Post emergency numbers on all telephones. Do not place your name on your mailbox. Maintain good external lighting. Control vegetation around your house to eliminate hiding places and to maintain an unobstructed view of windows. Exterior doors should be solid and should be locked with dead bolt locks and one-way peepholes. Glass doors and ground floor windows should be metal grated and have locks not reachable from the outside.

When you are away from the home for a while, make sure the house looks "lived in". Stop deliveries, or have them delivered to a neighbor. Use a timer to turn lights and radios on and off. Notify the police that you will be away, and if possible, have a neighbor or relative check on your home periodically.

These common sense precautions are good not only for protecting against terrorism but for providing security against other attacks as well.

Finally, should it be pointed out that anti-terrorism planning is a management as well as an individual responsibility. Management should work closely with local law enforcement agencies to ascertain that an anti-terrorism plan is in place and that employee's have been properly educated as to their individual response.

The preceding precautionary steps were anti-terrorist actions in which individuals can take to limit their vulnerability. The following represent counter-terrorist actions which are mostly likely to be initiated by Government organizations. Recognize that these actions are aimed towards the United States.

- The President should repeal the executive order against assassinations. If we are able to hunt down a terrorist, our agent should be able to kill him.
- Appoint more sky marshals and travel marshals. (If the Italians had a couple of marshals on the Achille

Lauro, the murderers probably could have been stopped.

- Develop short-term economic sanctions that might be usable in certain circumstances.
- Develop a package of training and provide assistance and equipment to friendly countries as required.
- Launch a diplomatic effort to isolate countries that support terrorists.
- Identify organizations that support and provide funding to terrorists groups and seize/freeze their bank accounts.
- Deploy some of our anti-terrorist Delta Force outside of the United States. There may be occasions when we'll want to use them immediately.
- Bolster our covert intelligence capability. We don't know enough. We are still paying for the emasculation of the CIA in the '70s. Also, we were surprised when Iraq invaded Kuwait.
- Ask the television industry to see if it can develop a code of self-restraint in dealing with terror incidents. Other professions have self-policing codes. We don't have to be on the air about terror every minute of every day.
- Consider covert or direct strikes against non-Soviet regimes that encourage terrorism: Libya, Iran Syria, Iraq, the Palestine Liberation Organization.
- Get very tough, very fast, on terror in America.
- Stop the turf wars in the U.S. bureaucracy. Appoint an anti-terrorism czar to knock heads at State, Defense, Justice, CIA, and FBI.

- Convene an international conference to share information and discuss ways to combat international terrorism.

It should be noted that, after the Oklahoma City bombing, the U. S. Senate passed a sweeping anti-terrorism bill, supported by the President that would bar organizations linked to terrorists from fund-raising in the United States. In addition the bill makes it much easier to deport terrorist suspects and streamline death-penalty appeals. Unfortunately, the bill is bogged down in the House, where House members (left and right) backed by the National Rifle Association and the American Civil Liberties Union believe the bill would provide too much power to Federal investigators.

Note:

The State Departments annual list of countries alleged to sponsor terrorism include the same seven countries as last year - Cuba, Iran, Iraq, Libya, North Korea, Sudan and Syria. (Consideration is being given by the State Department to remove Syria from the list).

Five years after the Oklahoma City bombing, the National Commission on Terrorism appointed by Congress has issued it's report which states that the United States faces a heighten risk of devastating terror attacks and the Government needs to do more to guard against them. In addition, while rightfully concerned about the security of it's foreign embassies, the Government should sharpen it's counter-terrorism efforts abroad and focus on the heightened risk of serious terrorist incidents at home.

Chapter 4

Vehicular Evasive Actions And Attack Recognition

Most terrorist attacks have taken place in areas where there are side streets. Knowing this can work to your advantage.

If you have an indication, that you are being followed and are in danger of being attacked, take evasive action immediately.

Make an unscheduled high speed turn in either direction to confirm you are being followed.

If following continues, seek a safe haven. If equipped with a radio, request help.

Keep windows closed in case Molotov Cocktails are thrown. If hit by such a fire bomb, either drive away at high speed, or if the vehicle is blocked, wait 10 seconds and abandon it on the opposite side of the fire. Such fire bombs normally burn out within a few seconds.

If attacked, have passengers place themselves below the window line of the vehicle. A 9mm and .38 caliber bullet may penetrate the normal auto body; however, the bullet might be deflected and its force reduced to a degree which will improve the survival chances of passengers. Use of body armor, an armor coat, or armor blanket will further increase survival chances.

If it becomes necessary to jump a curb, median strip, or traffic Island, it should be done. Enter at an angle of not less than 30 degrees and not more 45 degrees. Be prepared for a jolt.

HIGH SPEED TURN AROUNDS:

Used to rapidly turn an automobile 180 degrees using controlled skidding techniques. These procedures are especially valuable in avoiding road blocks. (See figure 3)

Types:
"J" Turn or reverse 180

- Stop the car, put it in reverse.
- Accelerate to 15-20 mph. Then lift your foot from the accelerator.
- Turn the steering wheel quickly toward the open lane.
- Front wheels will lose traction causing the front of the car to spin around.
- Keep off the brakes throughout the maneuver.
- Shift into low gear.
- Accelerate.

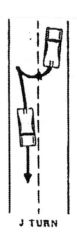

J TURN

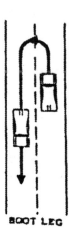

BOOT LEG

Figure 3

The secret of f a good "J" turn is the rapid turning of the steering wheel after lifting your foot off the accelerator and then getting back on the gas quickly. If done correctly, the "J" turn can be accomplished in a single lane, using just two feet more width than the car's length.

Bootleg or forward 180:

- Apply emergency brake, hard.
- Rear wheels will skid.
- Turn wheel slightly in the direction you wish to turn, usually to the center of the road.
- The rear of the car will spin around.
- Straighten wheels as the rear of the care comes around.
- Release emergency brake.
- Accelerate.

Prior to trying this maneuver, insure your emergency brakes will lock both rear wheels. Test your emergency brakes by applying them while moving at 5-10 mph on dry pavement. Both rear wheels should lock. Quite often, they won't or only one may lock, usually the left rear. The turn can still be done, but you must turn the steering wheel away from the wheel that is skidding. Never turn the wheel more than about 90 degrees. If you do, you will not make a clean turn, and may even go off the road if your rear wheels do not fully lock.

The bootleg is more effective than the "J" turn due to more motion of the car and the fact that the car never fully stops at any point. This technique needs slightly more room than the "J" turn.

Remember: **WHEN PURSUED BY POTENTIAL ATTACKERS, CONCENTRATE ON WHAT'S AHEAD, NOT YOUR PURSUERS.**

Know where your are going, preferably on a pre-planned escape route toward a safe area or haven. If there is a radio in the vehicle, contact authorities and tell them where you are going and the status of passengers and vehicle (i.e. injuries, care damage ect...)

If you are very close to the barricade or do not have room to make and evasive turn, you may have to ram through the barricade. Most barricades will consist of a car across the road in front of the victim. The proper method of ramming is as follows:

- As you approach the barricade, evaluate the situation, pick a possible ramming point, and if you have determined that it is an attack, slow the vehicle as if to stop. You must make the attacker think you are going to stop at the barricade.
- When you are about one or two car lengths from the barricade, floor the accelerator, striking the blocking vehicle at front or rear aiming your left or right fender at the axle center line. Strike either end of the blocking vehicle. Do not broadside the vehicle. Keep the accelerator on the floor until well past the barricade. Hold the steering wheel straight, do not swerve away at the last moment before impact. You will be going no more than 10-15 mph. More speed will damage your vehicle to the point that you may not get away.
- Beginning the run too far back will let the attacker know what you are planning. You will also build up too much speed. At the recommended speed, you will feel hardly any shock. The barricade

vehicle will spin violently out of the way. Anyone standing near the barricade may be hit.

- If the blocking vehicle is much larger than your vehicle, move your attack nearer the end of the blocking vehicle and start your run tow care lengths away. The blocking vehicle is sitting on four patches of rubber barely larger than your hand. As soon as you strike the blocking vehicle, it will break away. Very little force is required to keep it moving.

The element of surprise is most valuable in this technique. You will be able to ram through the center of the two vehicles or around the end, jumping a curb at the same time. The important thing is not to drive around the barricade without disturbing it in some way. This leaves you open to broadside fire.

There is also a tendency to steer away at the last moment and to lift off the accelerator. Ramming is a last resort technique when you are sure you are under attack, and there is no time or space to use another technique.

Making the determination that you are under attack may be the most difficult decision a driver may ever face. Events may escalate so fast that while you ponder your decision, the attack will have taken place. Recent attacks have been initiated within two seconds of the time the driver stopped. This means your actions must begin well back of the kill zone. In this span of time, you must decide whether or not it is an attack and which evasive action to take. You may use one or more of the following: escaping at high speed, "bootleg" turn, or ramming. You should then seek a safe haven as soon as possible. Deciding which tactic to use should be guided by the following:

- How close are you to the barricade?

- How strong does the barricade look? Can you ram through it?
- How fast are you going?   Fast enough for a "bootleg"?
- How much room is available, front and rear?
- Are the attacker's close enough for a accurate gunfire?

You should realize you are more likely to be attacked on a route that you normally take. Attacks are almost always preceded by an intense surveillance for planning purposes. The terrorist will find this hard to accomplish on any but your routing movements. You are also likely to be more inattentive on this route due to its monotony. All of this plays into the terrorist hands. During a survey of the route, you should catalog for each potential attack site, the type of attack, including the location of the nearest safe haven and medical facility.

Barricades have been used many times. The barricades may be disguised to look like a national guard or police identification check point.   If you have done your homework well, you will be getting daily information concerning where the official barricades will be placed. As you approach the barricades, you should make note of whether all vehicles are being stopped.   The barricade should look correct in every detail. Uniforms should be correct, and mot of all, the correct vehicles should be present.   Uniforms and barricades can be easily obtained, but the correct vehicles are much more difficult. If civilian vehicles or no vehicles are present, you should be ready to take evasive action. If you are far enough back, you may be able to simply turn around. If you are very close, you may have to ram.

Whatever the situation, quickly figure out the probability of such an action taking place. For example, when Hans Martin Schleyer was kidnapped in Cologne Germany, he was already the subject of a 24 hour police protective service operation. AS his motorcade rounded the corner one block from his home, he was attacked.

The terrorists used several ploys. First a VW van was posted in such a position as to prevent the follow car from swinging wide to cover the exposed left side of the principal's car. Then a female pushing a baby carriage moved off the curb in the middle of the block in front of the principal's. At the same time, a Mercedes sedan proceeded toward the principal's car. This Mercedes was traveling the wrong way down a one-way street. The Mercedes then cut in front of Schleyer's car causing the driver to stop.

The follow car ran into the back of Schleyer's car. The terrorists fired on the follow car from both sides and rear. They had been hiding in the VW van. The driver and passenger of the Mercedes jumped out and also opened fire on the follow car. The female pushing the baby carriage killed Schleyer's driver. Schleyer was taken captive and killed 43 days later.

Any analysis of this event cannot ignore the odds of a mother pushing a baby carriage in front of a moving vehicle. Very unlikely. The odds were also very small that in Germany, a locally registered vehicle would be driving the wrong way down a one-way street. In Germany, this is rare. The fact that it was now happening in front of a threatened person was even smaller. Everyone in the detail was killed on the spot. Schleyer was killed in captivity.

What the terrorist has planned to be very unobtrusive may be a dead giveaway if you are thinking. The attack will most likely take place where there is little traffic. It is difficult for a large group of people to make a getaway in bumper to bumper, stop and go traffic. The terrorist will need to insure that only your vehicle is stopped. This means that if it is to be done in heavy traffic, the terrorist will most likely be in a vehicle parked alongside your route. At your approach, they will have to pull out in front of your vehicle at a place where they have support personnel located in some form of disguise.

The weapons may be hidden in shopping bags for instance. The point is, the terrorists are in a mobile position and in the process of dropping their disguises. This gives you time to evade if you are ready for this type of attack. Study as many vehicle attacks as you can and spot the weaknesses of the terrorist positions. To survive, you must exploit those weaknesses.

The terrorist has just about every tactical advantage, numerical superiority, surprise, firepower, location, time of day and crossfire. To protect yourself against today's terrorist threat requires low profile and deception tactics along with effective route surveys and early attack recognition.

Rocket propelled grenades (RPG) have been used in several terrorist attacks. If your route passes open fields, wooded hillsides, or vacant buildings, these places could be used for RPG attacks. When the RPG is launched, there will be a large puff of smoke at the launch site. If the rocket missed, try to get out of the kill zone before another round can be loaded and fired. Wind affects the accuracy of RPGs significantly. The target must also be almost stationary. Beware of an unplanned stop near one of the sites you have picked as a possible RPG attack site. If you have a choice of routes, one of which passes a possible RPG attack site, make sure you stay away from the route on a still day with no wind; or, if you must take that route on a still day be especially watchful.

Whatever action you take, the important point is to do something. Take control of the situation. The attacker has observed you for sometime, and you have not noticed this and reported it. Otherwise, you would not be where you are. In other words, you are way behind and have a tremendous amount of catching up to do, with only seconds to do so. If you make one of the evasive maneuvers previously discussed, it may be enough to cause the attackers to break off. This is the best you can hope for. Without a doubt, your best chance of survival is to be alert for surveillance and report it promptly. Plus, <u>always be unpredictable</u> in your route and times.

Chapter 5

DO'S AND DON'T'S WHEN TRAVELING IN THE MIDDLE-EAST

In route by air, do not carry pornographic material (i.e. Playboy, Hustler, Penthouse or other x-rated magazines). Even newspapers like the Daily News and magazines like Newsweek have pictures of scantly dressed men and women that could get you in trouble.

Do not enter the country with alcoholic beverages in your procession.

Do not enter the country intoxicated.

Do not have drugs in your possession.

Do not talk to a women in which you are not a blood relative.

Do not lot look an Arab women in the eye. It is considered visual rape.

Do not walk or socialize with a woman who is not a blood relative.

If you travel with a woman by car, she must sit in the back seat and you (male) must act as the chauffeur. When you both reach your destination, you cannot walk together.

Women must wear a dress that covers them from neck to their ankles.

The dress must also cover their arms all the way to the wrist.

Women must wear a scarf to completely cover their hair.

Women cannot wear makeup in public.

In most Middle-East countries, you are not allowed to practice your religion in public.

It is not necessary for western women to cover their faces. However, their heads must be covered. Failure to comply with any of the above could bring about your arrest by the Religious Police (RP), who are extremely unforgiving to westerners. Women who are caught by the RP with their arms or legs not properly covered, will have their arms and/or legs spray painted. If their head is not properly covered, the hair will be cut or shaved. Arabs pray 5 times a day. When out in public and you hear the prayer music and singing from the local loudspeakers, you must get off the street and stay off until the prayer period has been completed. For women out in public, they should be aware of Arab men who like to touch (have hand problems). It's not uncommon for some Arab men to take advantage of western women by brushing up against them in public, pinching their arms, breasts or hips. If a women complains or makes a scene, then the RP shows up. Once the RP get involved, you have an Arab speaking Arab and you can bet he's not tell the RP exactly what he did. Most likely he'll say that the women propositioned him, he said no and now she's creating a scene. Unfortunately, the RP will believe that story, arrest the women for solicitation, stamp prostitute on her passport and have her kicked out of the country. It's also possible that she may receive a flogging before she leaves.

If you get caught stealing you will lose a hand. If you kill someone, you will lose your head at the chopping block. If you commit adultery, you will also lose your head at the chopping block. Friday is punishment day for any person(s) that committed a crime during the week. The Arab week however, is slightly different. The first day of the week is Saturday (our Monday), then Sunday (our Tuesday), Monday (our Wednesday), Tuesday (our Thursday), Wednesday (our Friday). Thursday and Friday (our Saturday and Sunday) is the weekend. You should remember this when traveling and avoid arriving in country on the Arab weekend as most facilities will be closed.

If you ferment a close personal friendship with and Arab (man to man/women to women only) you should be careful as to what private/personal bits of information you share with them. If you get into any type of trouble with the law and their necks are on the line, they will give you up in a heartbeat. The less they know about you and your business, the better. Also, there is alcohol in the Middle-East (American's have it). If you're socializing with Arabs, never offer them alcoholic beverages. If they ask for it, they will refer to it as "Tea and Kool Aid". If you invite Arabs to your house, make a room available for prayer with a window facing east towards Mecca. Finally, **DO NOT,** repeat **DO NOT** ever travel into the desert alone. However, if you do, be sure to carry the necessary survival provisions such as a radio, and/or cell phone, water, extra fuel, food, spare tire and cover for your head.
Final Notes:

1. Two Thai men convicted of drug trafficking were recently beheaded in Saudi Arabia. This brings the number of executions (beheadings) this year to 85. Last year (1999), at least 99 people were executed.

2. Recently, a Egyptian man had his left eye surgically removed in the first eye-for-an-eye punishment in Saudi Arabia in more than 40 years. The Egyptian male was convicted of of disfiguring a compatriot by throwing acid in his face. In addition to the removal of his eye, he was fined $68,000.00 and ordered to serve an undisclosed prison term.

3.   In Iran, if two people (male and female) have the hots for each other, there is a special law that will allow them to get married for a few hours and then get a divorce. Western's should not try this. The Iranian have already broken the law just for liking each other and not being legally married.

4.   OTHER TRAVEL SAFETY TIPS

- Do not joke about bombs of firearms in airport. (Penalty, jail and fine)

-Be on the alert for unattended packages and luggage. Report them to the Police or airline security.

-Do not accept packages from strangers.

-Don't wrap presents because they may be checked.

-Never leave a car unattended at the terminal.

-Keep photo ID handy as well as two pieces of ID.

-Do not pack flammable materials, fireworks, household cleaners or pressurized containers. (Violators subject to $27,500.00 fine)

-For international flights, be prepared to provide a contact name and phone number.

-To determine if you've being followed, change your pace.

-At your Hotel, leave shower curtain and closet door open when leaving the room.

-If possible, pick a room between the 2nd and 7th floor as most fire equipment cannot go beyond the 7th floor.

-Keep your room neat and orderly.

-Do not answer a page. Go to a phone in the lobby and call the front desk.

-If in the military, no uniforms off base.

CHAPTER 6

Ramadhan

1. Ramadhan is the fasting month for people of the Moslem faith all over the world. The Moslem Hijra Year has 12 months and each month has either 29 or 30 days. A Lunar Year has 354 days, 11 days less than the Western Calendar. Therefore, Ramadhan comes 11 days earlier every year in the Western calendar. Fasting is a must to every mature Moslem being able to fast. However, the following are excused:

   a. Sick or traveling individuals.
   b. Elderly people who may be adversely affected by fasting.
   c. Nursing mother.
   d. Females during their menstrual period.

Those who do not fast during Ramadhan must compensate for it by fasting an equal number of days later or by feeding poor people.

2. Mohammed, the Prophet, was born in 571 A.D. and died in 632 A.D. At the age of 40 (611 A.D.) he started his prophecy. In 622 A.D. (1 Hajra Year), he migrated (Hajara) from Mecca to Medina. The Moslem Year started from this date. In 624 A.D., Islam called for fasting, 13 years after the beginning of Islam. Fasting is one of the five basic beliefs of Islam, known as the Five Pillars of Islam. These Pillars are:

a. The two formulas of the confession of the Islamic Faith: God is one and Mohammed is His Messenger and Prophet. This is what is written on the Saudi Arabian flag.
b. Praying, five times a day (early morning, noon, afternoon, evening and late evening).
c. Alms giving (Al—Zake—H), around 2½% a year.
d. Pilgrimage to Mecca once in the lifetime, if it can be afforded physically or financially.
e. Fasting: The Koran makes it obligatory to all Moslems to fast during daylight for the whole month of Ramadhan, starting at the break of dawn and ending at sunset. Fasting involves total abstinence from food, drink or smoking of any kind. Ramadhan ends with a feast called Id—Al—Fiter (break—fasting) on the first day of the following month.

3. During the month of Ramadhan, shops in the middle-east open late in the morning, around 0900 hours, and close for the noon prayer, then open again around 1600 hours, close 14 minutes before sunset and reopen after the late evening prayer around 2100 hours for approximately another three hours. During the last 10 days of the month, most shops remain open in the evening until after midnight.
4. Being a quest of the country, you are expected to:

a. Be more patient and tolerant with Moslem employees during this month.
b. Refrain from eating, smoking or drinking in public during fasting time.
c. Refrain from smoking in your office or car in the presence of a Moslem during fasting time.

5. It is customary to extend greetings during the first week of Ramadhan to Moslems by saying "Ramadhan Mubarak" (Blessed Ramadhan). Also, you say to a fasting visitor "Ramadhan Karim" which means, I would like to offer you refreshment or cigarettes, but because you are fasting, I cannot.

Chapter 7

Code of Conduct/Guidance If You Are Subjected to Terrorist Captivity

As a result of sub par behavior displayed by some U.S. service members taken prisoner during the Korean War, the Code of Conduct was devised to provide guidance to service members who become prisoners of war. A spin-off from the Code of Conduct is the Code of Conduct Guidance Directive for Personnel Subjected to Terrorist Captivity.

Points of major interest and facts.

A. The DOD policy concerning the activities of service members when they are held captive by terrorists and hostile governments is to <u>survive with honor</u>. The guidelines relate to peacetime detentions in which terrorists or hostile foreign governments attempt to exploit service members and other captives to promote propaganda efforts, extract criminal confessions, obtain ransoms, or to discredit the United States and allied governments.

B. Military Government and civilian personnel have a responsibility to maintain faith in the United States and to assure other American captives that their government is making every effort to secure their release. By maintaining such faith, hostages effectively resist exploitation by their captors. In addition, service members should protect themselves from unnecessary punishment and harsh treatment by making every effort to remain calm and courteous, and to project personal dignity. Further, military personnel must protect classified information to the utmost of their abilities. Finally, to maintain organization, discipline, and moral strength among the captives, service members must organize under a chain-of-command to the fullest extent possible.

C. In addition to the above principles, the following guidelines apply to detentions by hostile governments:

1. Detainees should know that they are subject to the laws of the government where they are held captive.

2. Captives should be allowed to be placed in contact with the U.S. Government through the U.S.Embassy.

3. Military personnel should not attempt to act as combatants during peacetime detentions unless so ordered .

4. Service members should give their captor only that information required by the Code of Conduct. Detainees should provide name, rank, social security account number, date of birth, and the innocent circumstances leading to their detention. Further discussions should be limited to health and welfare matters, conditions of fellow detainees, and going home.

5. As stated previously, persons taken hostage should remain calm, courteous and project a sense of personal dignity. Aggressive or combative behavior should be avoided. Hostages should try to be viewed as a "person" (as opposed to a symbol) in the eyes of the terrorists. Avoid controversial or ideological conversation. Listen to the terrorist's

cause, but never pander, praise, participate or debate with them. Non-substantive topics, such as sports, clothing and family should be discussed.

6. Escape attempts may be made, but only after carefully calculating the chance of success, the implications of failure and the safety of captives who do not participate. Escape attempts should only be made if it is determined that escape represents the only hope for survival.

7. Detainees should avoid signing any documents or making any   public statements.

8. If possible find a place/surface to leave fingerprints.

9. A release means that the terrorists are losing control.

10. Always remember that the terrorist need you alive.

11. Do not give the terrorist a reason to make an example out of you.

12. If you escape, say nothing to endanger remaining hostages.

CHAPTER 8

Terrorist Revenge

When all is said and done, one could say that the act of terrorism is no more than an act of revenge. For example:

- The Israeli's bomb southern Lebanon in retaliation for a terrorist ambush against Israeli soldiers. The terrorist retaliated by bombing a tourist bus.
- A terrorist bomb kills a New Jersey woman and seven others. Yasser Arafat cracks down by ordering the arrest of followers of the two groups that claimed responsibility. But Militant Islamic leaders raised the specter of civil war by vowing revenge towards Arafat and new bloodshed for the Israeli's and the great Satan (United States).

Of course, the "why" of terrorist acts is not quite so simplistic as the revenge motive. There is a huge ideological gap between Arab terrorist organizations and the west, which represents the root cause of terrorist acts. France, to cite an example, is the chief supporter of the Algerian Government that is opposed by the growing in-country fundamentalist movement. The end results are terrorists attacks in France.

Let's us not forget the downing of an Iranian commercial passenger jetliner. The revenge factor resulted in the downing of the Pan Am commercial jet over Lockerbie Scotland.

Revenge is not a one-way street. It can backfire. Case in point....On July 21, 1973 the man Israeli agents had identified as Ali Hassan Salameh (The Red Prince) walked out of the Lillehammer cinema. He was accompanied by a blonde wearing a yellow raincoat. The young woman seemed to be pregnant.

They boarded a bus and got off at Furubakken Gate, a steep, quiet street. As they walked slowly up the street, a white Mazda suddenly pulled up beside them.

Two men jumped out the car. Salameh turned around and suddenly noticed the pistols in the strangers' hands.

The two men trained their guns on him and opened fire. Salameh collapsed, riddled by fourteen bullets. The killers dived into the car, which darted away from the scene. The blonde, untouched watched Salameh's life ebb away in a pool of his own blood.

The Red Prince was dead. (So they thought).

Then on July 23--the day when the Mossad should have rejoiced at the death of its vilest enemy--the news explode in the newspapers: the Israelis had killed the wrong man.

The man the Israelis had riddled with bullets was not Salameh. He was Ahmed Boushiki, a poor Moroccan waiter who had been living in Lillehammer for four years.

The blonde in his company on the night of the murder was non other than his Norwegian wife, Torill, who was in the seventh month of her pregnancy.

Another example of revenge gone bad, the United States bombed Libya in retaliation for a bomb attack at the Disco in Germany frequented by U.S. service members. During the attack, one of Khadafy's children was killed.

Egypt as a pro-western moderate Arab state with the United States as it's primary benefactor is also opposed by the fundamentalist movement. The end results are terrorist attacks against tourist as Egypt depends heavily upon the dollars that tourist bring in.

The Palestinian bomb maker, Yehya Ayyash, known as the "Engineer" was killed in the Gaza Strip recently when his head was blown up by a booby-trapped cellular phone. Within the Palestinian community, fingers are being pointed towards the Israeli security agency "Shin Bet". Israeli officials while welcoming the demise of Ayyash, as expected, the militant Islamic Hamas group immediately vowed revenge.

Some of the attacks, that Ayyash is believed to have planned are as follows:

April 6, 1994: Bus blast in northern Israeli town of Afula kills eight Israelis and a suicide bomber.

October 19, 1994: Hamas bomber Saleh Adel-Rahim al-Souwi kills himself and 22 other people in a suicide bombing on Israeli bus on Tel Aviv's main Dizengoff St.

November 11, 1994: Palestinian cyclist from Islamic Jihad kills himself and three Israeli soldiers at military post near Jewish settlement in Gaza Strip. Ayyash was thought to have tutored Islamic Jihad in bomb-making.

December 25, 1994: Palestinian police officer who is a member of Hamas movement blows himself up near soldiers' bus stop in Jerusalem, wounding 13 people.

January 22, 1995: Two Islamic Jihad suicide bombers kill 21 Israelis, all but one of them soldiers, at a bus stop in Beit Lid in central Israel.

April 9, 1995: Islamic suicide bombings kill eight Jews in two attacks near Jeris settlements in Gaza Strip. Palestinian leader Yasser Arafat cracks down on militant with arrests.

July 24, 1995: Hamas suicide bomber kills six people on bugs in Tel Aviv suburb of Ramat Gan.

August 21, 1995: Five people arc killed in Hamas suicide bombing of bus in Jerusalem.

November 2, 1995: Two suicide car bombers blow themselves up in the Gaza Strip, wounding at least eight Israelis.

In the climate in which we currently live, we can no longer afford to be dumb tourist or uninformed innocent bystanders. We must stay abreast of domestic events and keep a finger on the pulse of international events. If the Israeli's have just bombed southern Lebanon, maybe this is not a good time to visit Israel. If the Egyptians have just jailed some suspected terrorist, perhaps it is not a good time to visit the pyramids.

Some may be adverse to allowing world events to dictate or influence their day to day activities. This is a personal decision which must be reached with great consideration. The alternate would be to ignore world events and take your chances.

Note:

Some of the recent waves of terrorist bombings, that have rocked Israel have been called acts of revenge by Hamas for the death of bomb maker Yahya (The Engineer) Ayyash.

As this publication goes to print, the Israeli's have withdrawn from Southern Lebanon.

CHAPTER 9

Skyjacking

AIRLINE SECURITY

No airport in the world is safe from terrorist attacks. Security measures taken at most airports are largely insufficient.

The first concern of airline security procedures is to see that the passengers don't bring weapons or explosives aboard. The is why individuals must pass through a metal-detecting frame and put their carry-on luggage on a belt that passes through an X-ray device or is opened and inspected by trained security people.

Both the metal-detecting and X-ray devices are instruments whose sensitivity can be turned up and down. For practical reasons of passenger flow, the sensitivity is kept at a level that will detect a large metal object like a gun, knife or sharp-pointed screwdriver.

But what good are X-rays or metal-detecting portals against bombs made of plastic that weigh as little as a pound, yet are powerful enough to blow a hole in the fuselage of an airplane in mid-flight?

Unfortunately, the airlines put their trust in gadgets--metal detectors and X-ray machines--spending millions on equipment and little on the people who operate it. The machines can help, but they cannot make a judgment. Only a human being can do that, and Americans place the decision on whether or not a plane is secure in the hands of poorly trained, underpaid, unmotivated, overworked contract employees.

The secret of EL-Al's success is that it focuses on the passenger and not on the luggage. Security agents ask these questions at the counter: To whom does the luggage belong? Who packed the bags? What presents or gifts are you carrying? Who gave them to you? Where has the baggage been since you packed it? What are you carrying that does not belong to you--or that you do not know the contents of? The agent asks questions that cannot be answered yes or no. It gives him a chance to scrutinize the traveler for telltale signs of tying--the passenger's face becomes pale, lips tighten, Adam's apple bobs, or perhaps he begins to talk too loudly. If the passenger answers questions and satisfies the attendant that he is what we call kosher, then we are reasonably sure we have security.

Most security agents at U.S. airports are employees of an outside firm that won a contract because its bid was the lowest, not because the outfit provides the best security. At a major U.S. airport a security guard said he was responsible for X-raying all baggage at the international departures on his 5:30 a.m. to 1:30 p.m. shift.

He was obviously conscientious and hardworking, but no one could carry out the enormous task assigned to him. During his eight-hour shift he was given time off for lunch and a coffee break. The rest of the time he ran the X-ray machine. But no human being can watch a screen for the many hours and still do an adequate job. No one should watch for more than 20 minutes at a time--after that a person is not longer alert.

Unfortunately, airline security in the United States, leaves a lot to be desired. What little is being done to protect passengers is not done well. The U.S. carriers are spending enough money, but they are not spending it on the right things. The carriers follow FAA regulations, but these aren't tough enough. Security pays for itself in decreased insurance fees and increased ridership, but airline executives have made security a low priority. There is no reason to believe this will change until there is a major disaster at an American airport.

There are a number of relatively inexpensive changes that U.S. airlines could make that would greatly increase security:

1. Eliminate curbside check-in and match all bags to passengers.
2. Station security people--not just ticket agents at check-in counters-to ask questions and divert suspicious passengers. The ticket agents' job is to get people on the flight, not to keep them off.
3. Mark each bag after it has gone through security--and make sure only those bags are loaded.
4. Have special seats on board for suspicious passengers where flight crews can monitor them.
5. Keep non-passengers out of domestic and international concourses.
6. Isolate passengers on connecting flights coming from airports where security is weak and send them through security again.
7. Have one security system for the entire airport. At present, as many as four or five different agencies work the same terminal with little or no coordination.
8. Raise the caliber of security people. Choose bright, educated people, train them well, test them frequently and pay them a decent wage. At minimum wage, you get what you pay for.
9. Perform preboarding security x-rays on all domestic luggage as well as international. But never rely on them exclusively.

10. Take responsibility for security out of the hands of anyone involved in day-to-day flight operations. The security director should have the power to postpone or cancel any flight.
11. No piece of luggage should be left for more than a few seconds without attracting attention of security agents. The planted suitcase bomb is one to the easiest and commonest types of terrorist attacks, and dealing with it should be part of basic security. In Europe, where there are more terrorist attacks, it is a high priority. At London's Heathrow, speakers on the public address system warn passengers in public areas at 10 minute intervals not to leave bags unattended. In America there doesn't seem to be an awareness among security people that seemingly abandoned luggage could pose a threat.
12. New security alert over key-chain guns. A tiny key chain that apparently can fire two .31-caliber slugs is the latest in a series of low tech but deadly James Bond-style secret weapons to spark concern among police and airline officials.

Police agencies worldwide are adding the 3-inch threat, which costs $20 and looks like a common key chain, to lists of similar so-called disguised weapons that endanger airline security. Already included are pistols hidden in pagers, cigarette lighters, belt buckles and pens.

The key-chain gun is made of metal but can easily avoid detection at airport security checkpoints because travelers usually dump their keys into small baskets before passing through metal detectors.

The key chain apparently is designed to fire gas or signal shells, and Interpol technicians have not tested it with bullets. But experts believe it can function as a gun.

The Federal Aviation Administration, which regulates the airline industry and aviation security, said it learned of the weapon earlier this year from Greek officials and notified U.S. airports and carriers.

The key-chain gun, which apparently is made in Bulgaria, is readily available in Southern Europe.

Authorities first seized the weapon last year in Perth, Australia, and Athens. It also has been seized at Gatwick Airport n London. Like other disguised pistols, the key-chain gun is simple: It is cocked by pulling back the ring and fired with the touch of a button.

13. Airport bag scan is a bomb. New $1 million bomb detection machines are not living up to their promise, delaying efforts to screen all baggage for explosives.

Meanwhile, airlines have hindered Federal Aviation Administration efforts to test how effective the devices are by not sending all checked luggage through the machines. "Without improvements in performance, explosives detection systems may not ...ultimately screen 100% of checked baggage."

The $1 million machines are supposed to plug a gaping hole in airline security systems: the inability to detect plastic explosives, like the device that blew up a Pan Am jet over Scotland in 1988. X-ray machines cannot detect plastic explosives.

Awaiting the detection machines, airlines this year began profiling passengers, using a series of criteria to determine which people should be singled out for further examination.

The federal government is spending $68 million to install the machines at airports but, they are not working as well in airports as they did during their preliminary tests, and airlines are reluctant to use them.

The Department of Transportation ordered more tests earlier this year after a January report by FAA, and the inspector general found the airlines and couriers were ignoring regulations.

The report found that security was so lax that 10 packages loaded with 50 pounds each of pesticide slipped by airline personnel in Miami three months ago and weren't discovered until one burst as it was being loaded onto a plane.

In 1996, a ValuJet plane crashed in the Florida everglades, killing all 110 people on board. Investigators say oxygen canisters ignited or fueled the fire that caused the crash. A year later, seven oxygen generators were shipped aboard Continental Airlines flight in violation of rules imposed after the Valujet crash.

14. The Most Dangerous Airlines in the World. Based on the number of fatal accidents per million flights, the five airlines with the worst records over a 20 – year period (excluding terrorist – related deaths) are … Turkish Airlines (24.48 fatalities per million passengers) … Air India (21.48 fatalities) … Avianc (5.93 fatalities) … Nigeria Airways (5.53 fatalities) … LOT Polish Airlines (4.55 fatalities).

15. The Most Dangerous Airports in the US. Security at Major US airports is very poor. Terrorists who are bent on breaching US airport security have ample opportunity to do so in many US cities. Examples:

- Los Angeles International airport. It is possible to walk through several areas marked "authorized Personnel Only: without being questioned.

- Washington Dulles International Airport. Civilians without ID badges have been able to breach secured zones and walk onto the tarmac close to berthed airplanes.
- San Francisco International Airport. A determined civilian can easily walk through unmarked doors in the terminal, past airline gates, and onto the tarmac among airplanes of numerous different airlines. In one incident, a magazine reporter deliberately failed to show up for a flight to Seoul, South Korea, but airline security didn't notice, and his baggage remained aboard the aircraft.
- New York's JFK International Airport. A civilian can walk onto the tarmac at several locations at this huge airport. In one experiment, and unauthorized person wandered among large aircraft for 10 minutes.

Added airport gear Will "help expose explosives"

16. The Federal Aviation Administration is buying 60 high-tech machines to detect explosives at airports.

The announcement of a $75 million contract yesterday with L-C Communications came just three days after EgyptAir Flight 990 Crashed off Nantucket after departing from Kennedy Airport. The agency's move was touted on the same day an airline consumer group blasted the FAA for failing to boost airplane and airport safety.

It's the second explosive-detection system the FAA has ordered in the ongoing war to combat terrorism. These sophisticated machines use CAT-scan technology to detect a wide range of explosives while scanning passenger baggage.

In addition, the FAA has also proposed stricter safety standards and inspections of jet fuel-tank systems to prevent explosions on new aircraft. But Aviation Consumer Advocates state that the skies are still less safe because the FAA has not been proactive for passenger safety. "It's been 10 years since Lockerbie Flight 103 and the FAA has yet to build and adequate bomb-detection system". Some also question recent safety improvements touted by the FAA, saying that the new design standards for fuel-tank systems cover new not existing aircraft. It's also been charged that the FAA has failed to force airlines to install black boxes that record longer periods of cockpit voice and flight data. Another safety issue entails the FAA policy that permits more than jet to sue intersecting runways at the busiest airports in order to move more traffic, despite opposition from the pilots union. The FAA admitted the practice, but said pilots have a right to refuse simultaneous use if they feel it is unsafe. What if the passenger's feel it's unsafe?

NEW AIRPORT SCANNER

The latest high tech equipment in use by security personnel at airports is called the BodySearch and it can make out everything from the shape of your navel to the hairs on your chest. Developed by American Science and Engineering, the $140,000.00 scanning machine can peep under clothes and a few millimeters beneath the skin. Unfortunately, the machines have alarmed the privacy experts who see problems if used by the wrong people, as the device is extremely intrusive. Unlike a regular x-ray machine that shows the mere presence of metal, this device well create a permanent image given the choice of going through BodySearch or being patted down. Passengers are picked based upon the customs inspectors suspicions that the passenger could be carrying contraband. Passengers who choose BodySearch must sign a consent form. Hence they are lead to a private room to be scanned. To-date, most of the passengers selected have stated that they have no objections to the machines.

NOTE: Since I started this book, I've made several trips by air and I've noticed a marked improvement in overall airport security. Ticket agents will now ask you, did you pack your bags, and did anyone approach you to ask you to carry something for them in your bags? In addition, agents are requesting a photo ID. Also, there are signs and announcements stating that bags should not be left unattended and cars also are not to be left unattended at departure and arrival curb-side. These actions alone do not solve the airport security problem(s). However, it is a welcomed start.

HOW TO RE-ACT TO TERRORIST DURING A SKYJACKING.

It is at the beginning of a flight that the hijackers are most primed. They are at their emotional peak. They must make their move soon in order to take advantage of a fully fueled aircraft that increases their alternatives for diverting and redirecting the plan if that becomes necessary as landing rights are refused.

At the same time that the terrorists are at their emotional peak, the passengers are relaxed, glad to be on their way. Thus the terrorists and the passengers are at opposite ends of their emotional cycles, one peaking, one relaxing. That makes it so much easier to create the panic that leads to control.

If you are ever caught in a hijacking, I would urge you to observe the following recommendations.

1. Do not look a terrorist in the eye. Terrorists may interpret eye contact as resistance and pick you for a ritual sacrifice.
2. Do not be belligerent in anything you say or do. For instance, if you are a large man, keep in mind that many terrorists are small in stature and the mere act of your standing up unexpectedly might seem a threat to them.
3. Don't try to intimidate a terrorist. Some people when stopped by a police car will allude to "pull" or influence they have or how important they or a relative are. Don't ever try that on a terrorist, because the more "important" you are, the better you serve their purposes as a potential victim. On the contrary, try to be as inconspicuous as possible Don't ask questions of the hijackers. If the hijackers speak to you, keep neutral; don't try to

patronize them by pretending to be on their side politically; at the same time, don't say anything against them or their cause. Be polite, but try not to be subservient.

4. Hijackers are near-paranoid in their suspicions, so try to avoid conversation, even whispered conversation, with other passengers. It is extremely dangerous to confide in another passenger, however friendly they may seem. When exposed to danger, another passenger may trade your confidence in the usually false expectation that he will be treated well for ratting on you.

5. Some hijackers rob passengers of their valuables. Don't plead to retain something for "sentimental" reasons. They'll take it anyway and you'll only have made yourself conspicuous.

2. Always ask permission of one of the hijackers before getting up, changing your seat or going to the lavatory. If they refuse permission, it may be because they do not understand you. If someone does not translate for you, keep calm and try again later with another of the hijackers. Minimize your intake of coffee, tea, water or other beverages to avoid unnecessary trips to the bathroom Never forget that rising fear has an effect on the bladder. If the unlikely event that the hijackers offer you an alcoholic beverage accept it but avoid drinking it. You will want to have 100% of your wits about you all the time, even though you are trying to be passive and inconspicuous.

3. During a skyjacking, do not talk to other passengers, especially if you don't know them. This is important for the following reasons:

   - A stranger sitting next to you may be one of the terrorist (called the sleeper).

- If you confide to another passenger regarding a weapon you may have or a possible plan to over come the terrorist, that passenger may report you to the terrorist in an attempt to gain favor.

8. Take guidance from the flight or cabin crew. While they have not been trained in hostage rescue operations, most airline crews have received instructions on procedures to be following during a hijack.

9. It is important that you think correctly instead of lending your self to panic. You should know that once the terrorists achieve control over the body of the people on the plane nothing happens immediately. Your most frightening enemy can be time. Therefore think days instead of hours. Remind yourself that you and your fellow passengers are not alone. By that time millions of people around the world are with you, hoping for your relief.

10. If relief comes in the form of a rescue by a rapid response team on the ground, the moment you sense this is happening get down between the horizontal rows of seats and stay there. Do not let your feet get into the aisle. Do not sit or stand up until ordered to do so by the assault team.

PRECAUTIONS.

While not all inclusive, the following represents some precautions, you as an individual can take before your trip and at the airport.

1. Make a note of your passport number and the date and place where it was issued, and put this information someplace other than a wallet or

handbag since these might be taken from you. This will assist your identification after the hijacking is over.

2. If you have ever traveled to Israel and your passport has been marked with an entrance or exit stamp,. You may want to take the precaution of getting a new passport. The Israelis, incidentally, will avoid tamping your passport if you ask.

3. Most travel agents will supply you with a typed itinerary. If you leave a copy with a member of your family or friend, be certain to advise them not to release this information to anybody unless they are sure the information won't fall into the wrong hands. Do not keep you itinerary with your plane tickets if there is some destination on it that might give a hijacker the wrong idea.

4. Don't put medicines or anything else necessary to your health in your checked baggage. Keep them with you in y our carry-on bag or pocket of your coat. Keep prescriptions in the original bottle to avoid wrong-guessing by others.

5. Most Muslims react adversely to your carrying alcohol or skin magazines. Leave such magazines at home, and if traveling a high-risk route, you might want to skip the duty-free liquor concession.

6. If you belong to a veterans' organization that might be considered controversial by terrorists, leave your organization ID cards at home. If you work in defense industries or the military, you might want to carry anything that would identify you as such in your checked luggage. Military personnel should travel in civilian clothes whenever permitted.

7. I have strong feelings about everyone being entitled to read whatever they want, but when you fly you might not want to have with you literature that is

anti-Communist, religious, or might be construed to have an Israeli or political connection.

8. For traveling, most people choose comfortable, loose-fitting clothing. That's fine, but also use another criterion. You don't want your clothing to make you conspicuous.

9. You don't want to hang around an airport unnecessarily; so check with the airline before you leave home to make sure the plane is still scheduled to depart on time. If curbside luggage check-in is available, use it so that you don't have to line up at a ticket counter for a long time. Don't hang around exposed public areas. If you have to wait near the gate area, stay away from large glass windows, and face away from such windows. If you have a choice of seats in a waiting room, don't sit next to a waste-paper' repository or near any luggage that doesn't seem to belong to someone. A phone booth should be looked into before entering; if there's a package in there notify airport security.

10. In the unlikely but possible case that you hear a bomb warning given, follow the instructions immediately. If no instructions are given, get down flat on the floor. And do that immediately if you hear gunfire or explosions anywhere nearby. Do not scatter and run in panic--bullets will win every time.

ASSAULT TEAM RESCUE.

Regrettably, there haven't been enough skyjack rescues to give anyone a warm fuzzy feeling that one was about to happen. At any rate, in the event you are a passenger aboard an airline flight that's been skyjacked by terrorist. You need to know that most countries in the world have a

Delta Force or Assault team especially trained for airline rescues in the event negotiations fail and an opportune situation presents itself. If the go-ahead is given for a forced entry by the Delta-Assault team, the following sequence of events most likely will occur.

- Time permitting, the Delta/Assault team should be on the ground before the skyjacked airliner lands. (In flight rescues only in the moives)
- The area around the skyjacked plane after it lands should be sealed off.
- Local law-enforcement personnel via prior arrangements by Government leaders will be kept away. (Must avoid turf battle.)
- Delta/Assault team members will

  - Set up a surveillance group
  - Take positions around established perimeter
  - Make a concealed approach to the plane under cover of darkness and from the rear (blind spot).
  - Drill holes in the skin of the airliner
  - Insert fiber optic video cable to enable the surveillance team through sight and sound to identify the skyjackers and keep track of their movements.
  - All information will be passed to the actual assault team.

The surveillance group has now identified both the layout of the explosive devices and just before the assault, the position of the terrorist who, by his actions or words, will seem to be the one charged with detonating the explosives. Heading off such a detonation by shooting the would-be detonator becomes a high priority for one of the assault-team members first entering the plane.

For the assault, the team members wear balaclavas, showing only their eyes and mouth. They also present a fearsome spectacle to the terrorists. When seconds, count, it all matters. They are dressed either all in black or in dark camouflage outfits. Each man is equipped with a 9-mm. Browning pistol (or sometimes a Sig-Sauer or Walther PPK) with low velocity ammunition, ideally suited for firing in a confined space without loss of accuracy but with minimum danger of exiting from a terrorist's head or body and wounding or killing a passenger.

As soon as the entry point or points are selected, the assault-team members get their individual assignments. A frame charge made of Dartcord-type flexible lead-cased shaped explosive would be used. It is applied to the outside of each door and ordinary masking tape. A 10-second fuse is attached to the detonator. The charge is designed to fracture the frame of the door, blowing it inward but not across the fuselage where it could harm passengers.

The first man in throws himself immediately down on the door, and the leapfrogging begins. The next man in is the stun-grenade expert. The stun grenade is hurled in a predetermined direction based on the intelligence from the surveillance group. Naturally, the intention is for all the hijackers to be temporarily blinded and deafened by the stun grenades. The grenade hurler will then fall flat so that the rest of the assault team can literally run right over his back.

One man will have been assigned to head straight for the cockpit to shoot the terrorist leader. All of these men are trained to fire killing shots in rapid succession. The men who come crashing into your plane are experts. They have rehearsed the assault dozens of times to get their timing down to half seconds. When they go in, they go in for the kill.

Once the terrorists have been hit, the assault team gets out as quickly as it entered. The passengers are left to local law-enforcement and airline people. By the time the media gets a good look at the exiting hostages, the assault team should have vanished into the night.

- As a final note, if you hear an explosion followed by shots, you can assume the follow.

  - The terrorists are blowing up the plane and shooting passengers.
  - A rescue operation is underway.

Whatever you assume, get down low to the ground and stay there. Do not put the assault team in the position of determining if you are friend or foe.

During the successful Entebbe raid by the Israeli's, several passenger's were killed by the assault force because they were standing up. Get down--Stay down.

HEROES

If you should find yourself in a hostage situation, do not attempt to be a "hero". I know most of us are products of the "action hero" generation. The action hero list includes Rambo, Arnold Swarznegger, Chuck Norris, Jean Claude Van Dame and others. However, I cannot emphasis enough, "***do not be a hero***". Most terrorists have no regard for human life and do not share the same values as you and I. As such they are more than willing to die for a cause they believe in and don't mind taking you with them. If you should try for example to over-power a terrorist, you must consider the following:

- Re-action of the other terrorist (If you manage to over-power one terrorist, do you think the others will put down their guns?)
- Re-action of the passengers (You cannot assume that the other passengers will rise up and take on the other terrorist.)
- If the plane is on the ground (Your actions may hinder a possible rescue attempt.)
- If the plane is still airborne (Your actions may trigger a gun fight.)

If shots are fired and one round blows out a window, anyone in the immediate vicinity not bucked up will be sucked out (a horrible death). The plane will lose cabin pressure, oxygen masks will drop. However, since this is not rehearsed, some passengers in poor health may die from lack of oxygen. The plane will most likely go into a steep dive. The pilot may not be able to regain control. So, as you can see, a dangerous series of events can unfold as a result of one passenger attempting to be a hero, thereby putting the entire flight in peril.

As I stated previously, there haven't been many successful rescue efforts. You must maintain faith in the knowledge that an effort is underway to free you from the skyjackers. The rescue could be via political negotiations or by force.

CHAPTER 10

Terror 2000 - The Future of Terrorism

As we approach the 21st Century, what will future terrorist present to us. We could face the old fashion garden variety of terrorism (i.e., car bombing, ambush shootings, suicide bombings, assassinations and skyjacking) or perhaps even worse, terrorists could use biological weapons or make crude but lethal nuclear contamination devices using conventional explosives and radioactive materials easily obtained from medical laboratories.

Japanese authorities believe religious terrorists released a diluted form of the nerve gas Sarin in the Tokyo subway system. It could happen in the United States.

According to some reports, the cult was plotting to start a war between the United States and Japan.

Leader Shoko Asahara and most of his lieutenants are in Japanese jails on charges connected to the sarin gas attack in Tokyo, but the cult probably remains a threat to the U.S. Not all of $1 billion bankroll has been seized and some of the sect's more extreme members remain at large.

As part of a worldwide plot to build an arsenal of chemical and biological weapons, New York City cult members bought software to hack into computers at Long

Island's Brookhaven National Laboratory and used phony corporate cover names in unsuccessful efforts to buy laser components. They even downloaded information from the Internet on where to get the venom of the African green mamba snake.

Witnesses testified the cult sent agents to Zaire to gather information on the incurable Ebola virus and bought a helicopter and dispersal equipment in Russia for spreading anthrax and other biological toxins. They also allegedly looked into buying a nuclear bomb.

"With the collapse of the Soviet Union, the United States has emerged as the sole remaining superpower." "Nations are unlikely to directly challenge our interests through conventional warfare. Instead they rely on indirect aggression, the ideal weapon being cheap, effective and deniable--in short, terrorism."

"Religious terrorists give no quarter because they are carrying out God's will and contending against the 'forces of darkness."

Ethnically motivated terrorists are almost equally driven. "The ethnoterrorist is defending not only his family and his community but the memory of his ancestors, his cultural heritage and the identity of his people, many of whom have suffered and perished simply because of their ethnic affiliation."

In addition to religious and ethnic terrorists there are "gray area" terrorists -- criminals who use terrorism to squash opposition. The narcoterrorists in Columbia and crime families in Italy are examples. Both have murdered judges and carried out other terrorists acts, resulting in thousands of deaths.

State sponsored terrorism is still a problem. The next decade will see fewer, but more deadly, incidents of state-sponsored terrorism. Because of the deniability factor in terrorism, "false flag" terrorism will increase--acts committed by one nation in a way that implicates another.

No matter what their motivation, the ability to wreak devastation is increasingly available to small groups and madmen.

"A terrorist in a high school lab could make Sarin, which paralyzes the respiratory system." "Biological agents form another threat. Pulmonary anthrax is 99 percent lethal. A few grams could take out a major office complex. Viruses like Ebola and hanta -- the deadly hemorrhagic fevers that cause bleeding from every opening -- are even worse."

Improvised nuclear contamination devices are another threat. "If the World Trade Center bombers had packed their van with radiological material along with the explosives they used, they might well have rendered New York's financial district uninhabitable for decades to come."

Terrorists could also cause havoc or disruption by using computer viruses and other means to electronically loot bank accounts, alter financial records and commit assassination by computer by altering medical records. Other acts of mass destruction could involve the electrical grid, the gas pipeline system and the air traffic control system.

These horrific scenarios beg the question of how can the United States or the world fight terrorism without violating its citizens' rights. In 1985 Vice President George Bush convened the Task Force on Combating Terrorism to define the scope of the threat and formulate counter strategies. I would suggest that a similar task force today would be a good beginning to fight the new terrorists.

The threat has changed in the past decades, so we need new definitions and strategies. It should examine all assumptions and have no sacred cows. The next step is to examine all Counterterrorism policies and see if they are still relevant. If not, we need to update them or develop new policies.

One policy change I recommend is for political figures to stop making pronouncements they can't back up. If you talk tough and then have to eat your words, it reduces your credibility to zero.

Another problem is excessive reliance on high-tech intelligence gathering such as signal intelligence or eavesdropping and satellite imagery.

Too often, the more exotic the means of gathering information, the more likely our policy makers are to believe the resulting data.

As a final note, it was recently disclosed by Germany that an international gang of smugglers had been peddling for $250 million nearly nine pounds of plutonium-239 from Russia -- quite possibly close to enough for a nuclear bomb. This time, the smugglers actually delivered more than half a pound of it to police undercover agents posing as potential customers.

The end of the cold war was the undoing of Carlos and of the Marxist ideology that motivated him, and it lifted the threat of global nuclear war. But it also unraveled the repressive security system that kept close check on Soviet nuclear weapons and the fissionable material that goes into them. Now paradoxically, freedom could soon give terrorists or the maverick states that support them the possibility of acquiring the massively destructive power they never had a chance of getting in a bipolar world.

As such, "Terror 2000" - The Future of Terrorism could be now.

N.Y. NUKE THREAT

SUMMARY

Terrorists are most likely to be successful when individuals are lax in personal security and follow predictable daily routines. Obviously, total protection from acts of terrorism is impossible, but COMMON SENSE AND PRIOR PLANNING CAN SIGNIFICANTLY REDUCE THE LIKELIHOOD OF SUCCESSFUL TERRORISTS ATTACKS.

Terrorists will strike frequently, without warning, and often against undefended and easily accessible individuals. They may detonate bombs; hijack aircraft; or assault, kidnap, or assassinate personnel. Senior ranking personnel must be especially alert to this threat as the terrorist may simply target any government representative - military or civilian - regardless of rank or position.

Bombs have been detonated in crowded public places; commercial aircraft have been hijacked and passengers held for exorbitant ransoms; diplomats, military personnel and business executives have been assaulted, kidnapped, and assassinated. There have been instances where criminals, confronted with impending capture, seize hostages and mimic the acts of international terrorists.

Terrorism is at bottom a form of warfare, and it is directed against The United States and its allies. It is unprecedented to argue that we should not defend ourselves against these kinds of hostility, or to help others do so on the specious premise that to do so is to violate the sovereignty of that nation from which the hostile action emanates. Sending a terrorist team across a border to attack one's neighbors is no different in principle from sending an army. To suppose otherwise, is to encourage terrorism.

The overall intent of this book was not to provide a tutorial on terrorism but to provide some common sense ideas on how an individual can protect him or herself from terrorist activities, survive a terrorist attack, survive as a hostage and in general, stay out of trouble while on travel. The United States has a multi-Billion dollar defense budget. However, if you become a hostage as a result of a terrorist act, do not hold your breath and wait to be rescued. To survive you will need to rely on your good judgment, common sense and your faith in God.

REFERENCES

1. Terrorists "White Papers" written by Fred C. Ikle, Former Undersecretary for Defense for Policy, dated 23 June 86.
2. New York Daily News article, Subject: Recent Mideast Turmoil, dated 5 Nov. 95.
3. New York Post article with Photos dated 26 July 95
4. New York Post article with Photos dated 26 April 95
5. New York Daily News article dated 10 Oct 95
6. New York Daily News article by Gale Rivers, The War Against Terrorism 9 June 86
7. The Monmouth Message, article written by Evelyn D. Harris. American Forces Information Service, Subject: Mass Terror: Today's Legacy of New World Disorder, 8 April 95.
8. Article written by Peter Probst and Museum Cetron, Subject: Terror 2000: The Future of Terrorism.
9. New York times article, written by Craig R. Whitney, Subject: Plutonium for Sale - Call 1-800 Terror
10. Life Magazine article written by Ray Salazar, Subject: The Next Bomb, dated March 89, Vol. 12, Number 3
11. New York Daily News Article written by Richard Sisk and Helen Kennedy, Subject: Japan Cult Had Base in City, dated 1 Nov. 95
12. Article written by the Army News service, Subject: On Guard Against Terror
13. New York Daily News article written by Gene Mustain, dated 18 Feb. 96
14. ICT International Terrorism News Archive (Feb 98 – May 00)
15. New York Post article dated 3 Nov. 99
16. New York Daily News article. Re: Terror Alert Warning, dated 6 June 2000.

17. U.S. Army training circular TC19-5, Bomb Threats, Aug 75.
18. Traveler Safety Tips; The American Hotel/Motel Association, dated 1995.
19. U.S. Army Bulletin; Re: Terrorism, dated Oct 1982
20. U.S. Army Memorandum; Re: Security Procedures Against Acts of Terrorism, dated June 1986.
21. Vehicular Evasive Actions and Attack Recognition, BSR Incorporated, undated
22. New York Post Article, dated 31 August 2000.
23. Daily News Article, dated 13 & 15 August 2000.
24. Daily News Article, dated 22 December 1999.
25. Daily News Article, dated 22 August 2000.

ABOUT THE AUTHOR

Born and raised in New York City. He Joined the US Army after High School in 1962 and retired from the Army after 23 years in 1985. He has been Married to wife Carolyne for 37 years with four children. (3 boys and 1 girl). He has one son in the Army and only daughter in the Navy.

Together with wife Carolyne, have been foster parents since 1991 and formally adopted youngest son Joshua in 1995 Has Bachelor's degree from Southern Ill University and Master's in Education from Temple. For the past 14 years has worked at Fort Monmouth NJ as a Tele-communications Specialist. Likes to read ancient history.

Printed in the United States
3785